LOOK AT HER SHOES

Even In Loss, A Love Story Is Always Worth Living

ANGELO CARILLO

Contents

Introduction

Congratulations on purchasing *Look At Her Shoes: Even In Loss, A Love Story Is Always Worth Living,* and thank you for doing so.

This book will not be your standard text on relationships. Everyone knows that having a solid emotional base and a partner to live the rest of your life with is the end goal, but we also know that plans don't always come together. Relationships can end for various reasons, but you shouldn't allow this to deter you from the happy ending that you deserve.

This text will cover how to relate to the opposite sex on more than just a physical level, the process of forging and maintaining a relationship, and dealing with and recovering from rejection should it not go to plan. We'll also cover following the correct lead and putting yourself in the shoes of the desired party in relation to forging a said partnership. You'll also find tips on working on yourself, maintaining your emotions, and knowing your worth that will help forge those relationships.

Lastly, this text will also stress the importance of forming bonds outside of your relationship, so you don't rely on it for all of your emotional needs. We'll also cover the emotional and communication aspects and why they are equally important to all your relationships that you'll have in life. The aim here is to help and nurture while also fostering healthy relationships all around.

There are plenty of books on this subject on the market. Thanks again for choosing this one! Every effort was made to ensure it is full of as much useful information as possible. Please enjoy!

Chapter 1:

Relating to the Opposite Sex

Before you can foster any strong relationship, you must find some common ground. It's no secret that a relationship cannot work if the two aren't compatible. In early courtship, this can fall by the wayside, which leads to the possibility of failure. In every instance, we are drawn by physical attraction. It's simply human nature for this, as we're always drawn to what our eyes deem beautiful. Though this isn't necessarily a bad thing, it can't be the be-all and end-all when it comes to relatability in a relationship. You have to connect on an emotional, intellectual, and communicable level.

Before we go into the three important relatability aspects, what exactly is being relatable? The bare-bones minimum definition is the quality of being easy to understand or feel sympathy for. Though these aspects are important in a relationship, you have to be relatable beyond understanding and sympathy. Both are a part of the emotional aspect; however, they only make up a very small amount. It's easy to understand and sympathize; to connect requires more input on your part.

Take, for example, on an emotional level. Sympathy, for the most part, is an easy emotion. Most can sympathize with someone's feelings or thoughts, but taking time and connecting requires more than this simple trait. It would be best if you listened for emotional cues and aspects. Women are more expressive with their emotions than men, so they're more likely to provide such clues. It's up to us to determine these cues and hone into the situation at hand.

Being able to listen to your spouse on an emotional level goes beyond just sympathy. You're taking into account their feelings and emotions and giving yourself to them to spill express everything on the table. Instead of giving them an "I'm sorry" and "I sympathize," you're asking to know how they're feeling and what's the next step. You're putting their needs first, which leads to a stronger understanding. Knowing this information is the first step to a natural and fruitful connection and will build a stronger connection. Showing this will add to your appeal, take you far in your current situation, and be fruitful should this relationship not go according to plan. Having this knowledge becomes key and can guide you in other relationships and bonds.

Being able to harness the right emotions at the right time is also impeccable. This aspect can make or break situations and often leads to misunderstandings that lead to further issues. During your initial courtship stage, it's important to know that you may not be the only person with her attention. Showing jealousy over this is normal but not the best emotion to show her in trying to court. This emotion can be positive, however, if you know to harness the situation. It's at this time when having a cool demeanor will work in your favor. If you can find ways to turn the emotion into determination for the goal, it will prove to be a fruitful process.

The most important of the three aspects is being communicable. In any relationship, there's nothing more important than communication. It doesn't matter if you're looking for a spouse, a friend, or if you're with family. The ability to talk things out works better than holding things in and being open works wonders in all aspects of life. That being said, being communicable is about more than just talking. You have to be a great listener as well.

The key to being a good communicator is the give and take. You have to be able to listen well and actively to provide to the conversation. Keeping this give and take action shows the ability to communicate. Not only that, but it shows that you're not dominating the situation but enjoying the moment. Listening also adds to building trust in the relationship. By lending your ear, you can learn so much from whom you are seeking. Being abreast of these moments is why active listening is imperative. You don't need to know every detail, but knowing the important moments, memories, and traits will be your best foot forward.

This instance in the courtship is when active listening will play a factor. Active listening is staying in tune with the conversation but also adding engagement. Doing this doesn't allow you to overtake the conversation but continue to add to it. It also shows you are in tune with your partner's interests. Active listening only adds to your appeal. Your partner will be more willing to open up about themselves, which builds trust and chemistry. You'll need both of these aspects to continue to grow in the courtship. Without these traits, a courtship is meaningless.

Having this option available may also be the opportunity for you to open up a bit about yourself. This aspect goes a long way to building that relatability. You'll find common interests or possibly something you'd never thought about before. Active listening expands your horizons as a future mate and as a person in general. It allows you to hear and see things from another person's perspective. This trait is important in the courtship stage as well as building bonds with friends. It also shows your level of maturity to maintain and engage. Having this trait in your back pocket will prove fruitful in all aspects and should continue to be built upon should you already have it. Don't let this slip away, as you'll need it for all of your social engagements.

It's also not about what you say in a lot of instances. It's more the meaning behind the words. Most people believe that being able to talk automatically means being able to communicate well. This thought process couldn't be further from the truth. Your words have to contain merit and emotion, not be empty and hollow. You can't speak just to be speaking; there must be meaning and gumption behind your words. Anyone can speak a bunch of gibberish about nothing, but being able to convey affection and proper emotion with your words and show intellect and keep the conversation moving makes you look better in the long run. These aspects will prove very fruitful in the grand scheme of things.

Now, that doesn't mean to stay quiet and allow them to dominate the conversation. This trait will be noticed quickly and will lead to awkward situations. You also have to display the active portion of the listening. Anyone can easily sit back and give a couple of nods and feign interest. Active listening also requires some retainment of what's being told. You're not expected to know every detail, but be in tune with the important memories and stories.

Be abreast of clues that will let you know of such importance. There may be a change in voice inflection, movements, mannerisms, or even slight eye movement. Paying attention to all of this is a part of active listening. It's not just talking but listening for all the senses and using those clues to your advantage. Knowing these clues and using them in action will show your interest in the courtship and help things progress further.

In communication, it helps be active. Engaging in the conversation keeps the journey of the courtship flowing. It's also a way for each of you to learn about one another, building that bond and trust that's needed. It's never easy to open up to someone new, especially if you are introverted. However, if you can't open up to anyone, it's going to be difficult to forge a true bond. That's why being a great communicator is imperative. You want to convey the right message and confidently but also engage and keep things active.

Keep in mind; you also don't want to make it all about yourself. It's important to share the conversation and not dominate it. During this stage, it's better to use a more open-ended type of speech. Using this technique allows her to open up more and gives you a chance to either follow up with a similar instance or engage in the topic given and learn more from her. This activity helps in bonding and building more trust in the relationship. Both parties should enjoy conversations, and making it about yourself comes off as selfish.

Communication is key in all aspects, but most importantly in the courtship stage. You'll never learn about someone unless you ask, and that requires talking. If you can't communicate effectively, then success will be difficult in the courtship stage. You have to be able to maintain a conversation but also not make it completely about yourself. Know the aspects of a great give and take in conversation and also use this time to listen. Being a great communicator is more than just talking.

It's not just what you say but how you say it. Don't have words that are empty and hollow; make them count. Anyone can do a bunch of talking about nothing. Being able to hold a conversation of substance will be the goal you're looking for. Go beyond the small talk that can dominate most conversations. You want to find something deeper instead of scratching the surface. This helps in building more relatability in the courtship.

Communication is also active listening and being attentive to your partner. Maintaining active listening will help with the give and take within the conversation and show that you don't want to make it completely about yourself. It's a brief expression of humility on yourself and interest in your partner. Showing this trait to your partner will also pique their interest in you. Remember, you don't need to maintain every detail about them, but knowing the important dates and memories is what you aim for. Use active listening as a part of your communication process, and you'll see how much easier relating will be. Talking is important, but listening and adding substance is what will get you the furthest.

The intellectual connection is often overlooked. This happens mainly due to focusing on physical attraction. One can't deny that appearance is important; intellectually connecting will be the bigger building block.

This aspect can go beyond just holding an intellectual conversation. It's also about picking up key vibes and knowing how to work with them. Being able to do this and continuing to engage requires a bit of intellect and timing.

Having both of these aspects reigned in will show that you're more than just a bit of eye candy, but you also can handle yourself in the courtship aspect with ease. This will raise her curiosity about what else you can accomplish and makes you a bit more desirable. All of this is done without engaging in any awkward conversations—a smart way to earn points and avoid unwanted situations.

Keeping in the intellectual theme, having knowledge, in general, is considered desirable. What is meant by this is having some form of enlightenment. Something you know everything about, and that can provide use. This doesn't necessarily mean you need to be the smartest man in the world, but have a common worldly knowledge shows that you are beyond the means that she may have been expecting previously. Keep in mind; you don't want to come off as arrogant or conceited. It's more or less just sharing something she may not have known to spark a conversation. Being armed with this gives a slight advantage of having a deep intellect that was once perceived. Having this will add to your mystique and may also pique her interest higher.

Beyond vibes, cues, and conversation, an intellectual connection can also come from shared hobbies and topics. This isn't a call to learn everything possible about your partner but to be abreast of what's important to her. Having this intellectual knowledge can only be a plus in your department. It allows you to have a near leg up in a lot of ways. By this, you can establish some common ground or even increase your knowledge by learning something new. This can also help in the courtship department as you're finding a mutual interest that suits you. You're also developing similar interests, which is a sign of compatibility. By engaging in this dialogue, you're finding another way to be relatable. You're also opening up more, which is building trust in the relationship.

In the end, it seems like a daunting task to try and relate to the opposite sex. However, it's all about putting in the good work and appealing to the aspects of relatability. This means communicating, assessing your emotions, and using your intellect to read situations and vibes. Having these instances in your back pocket will help foster a positive outcome to your goal in mind.

Remember, it's also important to listen while communicating and being abreast of the conversation's cues. Having the right reads and knowing when to communicate back will serve well in achieving the next step in courtship. You also don't need to dominate the conversation and allow the natural give and take to build the chemistry needed. This is one of those moments when humility is the key.

Active listening will be a key tool to possess during this stage. Know all the context clues of the conversation and key in on important events. Remember, you don't have to know every detail about the person, but knowing what is most important to them and retaining that knowledge builds trust and chemistry. Through active listening, you'll also find similarities, build trust, and even find new ideas you may not have thought of. Just maintain being active while listening and communicating. Not doing so will lead to awkward situations that you may not be able to save yourself from.

Lastly, don't forget about staying in tune with the emotional side. Make sure that you're concise with your feelings and avoid misunderstandings. Don't just be sympathetic to your partner's situation, but attempt to be one with it. You may never understand their full emotions, but showing that understanding and willingness to go beyond sympathy will show the scope of your emotional maturity.

In the same vein, know how to harness your own emotions to avoid any misunderstandings. Holding on to the aspect will help avoid those situations and keep the courtship process on the right track. Though this aspect is always easier said than done, doing so will be fruitful for you, the courtship, and future friendships alike. Avoid awkwardness and keep a level head; otherwise, you may end up back at square one.

Keeping up with all these aspects will help understand the fairer sex from a much clearer perspective. Though this understanding will never be at 100%, at the very least, it gives some insight. It also helps build chemistry and trust, which will be useful moving forward. Use what you can to attain that relatability and understanding, as it will make moving on to the next steps easier. Furthermore, it'll help in gaining and maintaining the confidence to move forward in your courtship journey.

Chapter 2:

Finding Your Strengths

In the courtship stage, having that connection is important, as we stated in the previous chapter. Though connecting on an emotional, intellectual, and communicable level helps, you also have to throw yourself into the courtship. Doing so can be a daunting task, as you may not know what you can bring to the table. Most of us mistake what we bring as more materialistic items, such as money or a house. Having these things are nice, but that's not what makes you who you are. You have to look inside yourself and determine your strongest traits. In this chapter, we'll go over what traits to look for and how they will help you find your strengths in the courtship.

There are three aspects to look for when determining your strengths: physical, mental, and personality. Some of these you may even see as a weakness but maybe a strength in your current situation. It's all in how you use that particular trait. We'll go over each aspect in detail and determine what could be your strongest traits in each, further defining your strengths in the courtship and relationship stages.

When determining your positive physical traits, a lot of us think of appearance. This initial trait isn't a bad start, but we tend to go more negative than positive from here. Going this route puts you at an immediate disadvantage as it represents a negative image of yourself. Starting negatively will travel through the relationship itself, and it's an instance you don't want to follow you around. Having this feeling can affect your other relationships and bonds, which is also another aspect that you want to avoid. We'll discuss ways to avoid this aspect and even go over aspects where negativity towards those traits may not be warranted.

We're all hard on ourselves when it comes to physical appearance. Most would say we're our worst critics. We'll find the smallest instances about how we look and focus on the negative about them. We also allow these negative thoughts about ourselves to find their way into our courtship aspects. Instead of leaning into these quirks, we find ways to hide or minimize them. Examples may include wearing loose clothing to hide our bodies, finding ways to alter our bodies, wearing caps or wigs to cover balding areas, using dyes to cover gray hairs or various other ways to hide blemishes and "unsavory" features. However, these quirks may not be seen as negatives and could be used as a strength in your favor.

Most men seem to believe that having the perfect body gives them a leg up in attracting the opposite sex. Yes, having a fresh set of abs and nice arms may catch some attention, but many women also enjoy a heavier set male figure. In today's age, the "dad bod" has made an emergence as the preferable male figure. This body type isn't one that's chiseled out of granite. Just like most men, women enjoy curves and something a bit softer to hold on to. Having a little extra works out in your favor. Embrace the body type that you have, as you never know who might enjoy the skin you're currently in.

Balding and thinning hair is also seen as a negative to most men. We tend to look at this as a loss of youth or an embarrassment. We often go to extremes to cover this up, normally with a wig a hat. You also find some individuals going as far as getting hair transplants. While having a full head of hair can be a turn-on for some, many women find bald or balding men attractive.

To some, this trait is viewed as a sign of maturity. It shows you aren't scared of what's coming ahead or worried too much about something so small. Not to mention the many actors and entertainers in media and television that rock the look. From Vin Diesel to Dwayne Johnson, it's a look that's become much more respected and revered. Don't be ashamed of that dome, sir!

One other seemingly negative trait is the appearance of gray hair. Most men see this similarly to balding or thinning hair. It's a sign of getting older and losing youth that was once held. This aspect, however, is seen as a positive to a lot of the opposite sex. Many women enjoy the salt and pepper look and attribute that to maturity, just like balding. Also, most women believe that an older man brings in more experience, so showing that you have that experience adds to your appeal. Keeping your gray hair also gives a confidence factor.

This aspect shows that minor details don't bother you, and women respect that. It shows that you have more of a cooler head and don't fear getting older. All of this leads to higher confidence and a stronger attraction to the opposite sex. Don't be ashamed of the grays or getting older, as this is a huge selling point for yourself.

Beyond these traits, we often look at smaller blemishes or unique marks on ourselves as negatives, whether it's a chipped toothed, larger facial feature, a birthmark, or other physical abnormalities. We allow these things to consume who we truly are. Even in these instances, they may be seen as a strength. It's a trait that's unique to you and makes you attractive. What you may see as something ugly, they may view it as a beautiful imperfection.

No one in this life is perfect; otherwise, we'd all be boring. Having something unique to you gives you the advantage of standing out in a crowd. Whether it is positive or negative is based on how you view it. If you turn that negative into a positive, it further shows your strength of character. It's a sign of maturity to see past your faults and let your true self shine through. Also, that added confidence to do so and own your appearance makes it that much more attractive. Furthermore, most women enjoy these imperfections. Never look down on yourself, as you never know who may like what's offered in front of them.

You may view abnormal physical traits as negative, but it's only if you allow them to do so. If you allow these traits to hold you back, then you'll be stuck in a rut in all aspects of your life.

Don't allow yourself to be hung up on the smallest of imperfections. Lean into and own them as a positive for yourself. Going this route will help build confidence and prove an added attraction than the perfection you are seeking.

Mental traits are a bit trickier as they can be misunderstood. These traits aren't an aspect of how your mind works but how you can mentally handle moments and feelings. Having a strong mind and keeping a cool head in situations can work wonders for you in the long. Whether it's in the relationship, courtship, or bonding, it's a very important trait. In this case, it's the mental stability to handle yourself. Having the right amount of vulnerability can also be important. One can only be so strong in a relationship, and there will be times when your partner will need you to confide in them. Showing this side of yourself helps build the trust element and leads to a bigger build in chemistry.

Now, one must understand that keeping a cool head does require patience. Not just patience with your partner but also with yourself. The ability to maintain yourself goes a long way when building relationships and bonds. There will be instances where you'll be faced with a situation that's not ideal. It can be an uncomfortable situation, an uncomfortable conversation, or general anxiety. It's during these times where your mental stability will come into play.

Will you panic, through your hands in the air, and give up on the situation? Or will you attempt to remedy the issue with keen sound and mind? The answer to this question will change the course of how your bonds are formed. You have to be able to be patient in these times and not make any inappropriate decisions. If you feel unable to maintain that stability, find a respectful way to excuse yourself from the situation. It's much easier to explain after cooling down than allowing the moment to dictate it for you. Try to avoid excusing yourself if you can, but use the out if needed. Your partner or friend will understand once you've explained everything.

Also, understand that this doesn't mean you can't be vulnerable. Friends and partners alike still want to be a shoulder for those that they find important. Just as they expect you to be strong for them, they will reciprocate. Everyone has ups and downs in life, so that vulnerable feeling will creep in ever so often. During these times, everyone needs someone to keep them afloat. You have to know when these times have risen for you.

From here, you have to decide to either open up about it or try to handle it internally. The choice of self-handling could backfire and show that you're not willing to communicate. Opening yourself up and sharing your vulnerability works twofold by building chemistry and enhancing trust. These two aspects are important in bond building, which we'll go over later. Knowing this is a strength early, however, will prove fruitful for the future. Having the ability to share yourself is a rare trait in itself, so hone this skill if you already possess it.

It's important to be on top of your mental state personally and know your breaking points. It's also important to be that open book to share those moments when necessary. You don't want to be viewed as too dependent, but you also don't want to be too stoic.

Personality traits are some of the best strengths one can have. These are your true self coming to form and how you are in everyday life. There are a plethora of these traits that all of us contain. Some of them we may even consider quirks. However, these also may work out in your favor and other personality traits that you possess. The best thing to do when determining your strongest traits is to start with some self-reflection.

Now, what does self-reflection entail? This process is looking inward to find what you believe best describes you. There are many ways to do this, though most wish to do so in the mirror. Seeing yourself in an image can normally help determine your mental and personality traits.

From here, it's determining what you feel you do best. Are you more talkative and outgoing, or reserved and shy? Does your voice carry over a room, or are you more soft-spoken? Is your attitude more flashy and abrasive or calm and quiet? How do you feel others see you in a public setting? These are just a few of the many questions you can ask yourself. These questions will give you the reflection needed to help you determine your personality and hone it to put your best foot forward.

You can also determine your personality through the very actions you take daily. If you have more of a routine for your day, it shows stability and structure. You have a certain way of doing things, and you stick with it, but this could also be seen as lacking spontaneity or, in lack of better terms, boring. However, not having a plan can also be viewed as lacking maturity and having no direction. Again, it's all in how you work this particular trait. If you allow it to be a negative for yourself, people will view it negatively. This is similar to your mental and physical traits.

Focusing on the negative aspects of your personality shows to others. Most do this with self-deprecating behavior masked as a joke. We all fall victim to it, but it's completely counterproductive. If you make yourself the butt of the joke based on shortcomings, it harms you in the end and makes you less desirable. Instead of using your humor against yourself, use it to make yourself the life of the party. It's turning the negative into a positive.

With your personality, do some self-reflection. Truly get to know yourself and determine what you do best. From there, avoid turning those determinations into negatives. Focus more on honing them into positives and lean into them as your physical and mental traits. Doing this will prove to add to the arsenal of traits needed to build yourself up. From here, you'll have the continued advantage in courtship and will have more confidence than you may have thought you had.

When going over your strengths, keep in mind the three aspects we discussed. Beyond that, really look at them from a larger scope. Don't immediately veer towards the negative and look at all the positive aspects of who you are. Starting your self-reflection in the light, and making your list from this perspective, will give you the strengths needed to move forward and continue in the courtship stage. Use these strengths to your advantage and know when and where to apply them.

From a physical standpoint, this is highly important. The majority of us like to go negative immediately in this aspect, which puts us at a disadvantage from the beginning. We all have this image of perfection that we need to overcome, as no one is truly perfect. It is these quirks that make us uniquely us. Lean into your quirk and use it as a strength, as you never know who may already view it as such. This goes for body image as well. Own the skin that you are in, and the results will follow. This will go a long way to making you that much more desirable.

Mental traits are essential for building chemistry and trust in a friendship or courtship. To build these, you have to know when to be strong but also when to be vulnerable. You have to know when to be that shoulder to cry on and know when you need the shoulder yourself. Being stoic all of the time can be taxing on you and the courtship you're trying to build upon. In the same vein, being too clingy can drive someone away. You must know the happy balance between the two or know which spectrum is your strongest.

Having all of these traits honed in will do wonders to extending your strengths. Armed with these aspects and knowing how to use them will give you the upper hand in courtship and friendship. These will be the building blocks to a strong foundation in trust and help form strong bonds. These traits will also help build your confidence to new heights, possibly finding things about yourself that you didn't know before. Be sure to have these in tune to be the best you possible, as being your strongest self will prove fruitful as you move forward.

Chapter 3:

Gaining Confidence

Now that you've determined your strengths, it's time to put them to work for you. In doing so, you'll begin to build another trait that may have been once seen as a weakness. You're may already be aware of the trait in question.

To continue a courtship and to blossom it into a relationship, it's going to require a bit of nerve on your part. Putting your best foot forward and showing what you can provide isn't always easy. The good news is, with the aspects we've followed in the previous chapters, you can use those to grow this trait and use it for future bonds and other relationships. This chapter will go over ways to help gain and maintain your confidence and the importance of having this trait.

Confidence, in a nutshell, is the way you carry yourself. It's also, through these actions, how others will see you. How you represent yourself is one of the main building blocks to confidence. If you don't truly believe in yourself and your abilities, then who will? Similar to finding your strengths, you'll use these tools to build your confidence. As stated before, knowing your strengths goes a long way to building that confidence.

Owning yourself for who you are is huge in being the best person you can be. Viewing yourself negatively will eat at you and kill any form of attraction you may have. Having this mindset shows in more than just appearance, but also tone. If you drive the narrative that you're less than worthy, then that's the vibe you'll give off. You're making the narrative true by enforcing it. It would be best if you got out of that mindset immediately.

With that said, this also means don't be full of yourself. It's great to be confident in who you are but also express some humility. No one wants to be with a person who views themselves higher than anyone else. This mentality will turn people away, as it shows hidden insecurity or an attempt to over-advertise yourself. You have to find an even balance when it comes to confidence—that perfect mix of owning yourself but knowing your faults. Having that balance not only shows an important level of maturity but also adds to your physical attraction.

With that being said, it's understandable that confidence isn't something that you gain overnight. A lot of men have issues with gaining and maintain that confidence. Especially over time, when everything seems like it's slowing down and getting older, the positivity once had in youth tends to wain. It's important to understand that this is normal, and during these times, it's great to do things to build that confidence back. You can achieve this by re-acquiring an old hobby, developing a new one, or finding a passion you've always wanted to try.

However, confidence is something that can be gained with the right amount of patience. It's more about how you view yourself and knowing your worth, but being humble about what you have. Maintaining that confidence also requires your effort. It's finding your best aspects and highlighting them without trying to outshine others, standing out, and making yourself known without putting down those who are also out there. You can't forget to maintain your humility, as having too high ahead can prove disastrous. Know the limitations of your confidence, but show it off when it's needed.

Confidence is a tricky trait. It's one of those that can work in your favor in some instances or lack in others. When it comes to relationships, this trait is normally in the latter department. This lack of confidence could be due to a shyness that you're unable to shake, fear of rejection, or some other underlying cause that hinders your ability. This issue happens with a lot of men, mainly the second reason. The fear of rejection alone can shake any person's confidence, let alone when dealing with courtship. You can't allow this fear to consume you completely, however.

A wise man once said that you miss 100% of the shots that you don't take. This philosophy is true in life as well as courtship. Living in fear of an unknown entity will keep you in the dark from a lot of experiences. This fear can even be harmful in embarking on relationships, as you're more afraid of what's going to happen instead of living in the moment. You can allow this fear to keep you from going after what you want. Even if you are denied, not taking the risk will leave you with more doubt of your abilities.

Not taking the chance automatically takes you out of the game. If you're looking to gain an advantage in any courtship, you have to make that move. Yes, there is a risk that you may be turned down, but you can't allow that to deter you from what you're looking for. If you choose to quit in this instance, it will be the failsafe you'll fall to every time you get to this point. You can't allow that fear to consume you, or you'll never take the chance of gaining the courtship. Instead, you're stuck asking what if or why didn't you try. Having those aspects of second-guessing will eat at you worse than the rejection itself. It'll stick with you through many other instances, and you may not even be aware of it.

Being stuck in a rut of fear can lead to a failure's mentality. It starts with the fear of getting into relationships but can also affect life decisions. Maybe there is a job that you know you're qualified for but don't have the confidence to apply for it. You missed that opportunity because you never took the shot. Or maybe there's an opportunity available, but you think you lack the ability even to attempt it. These decisions leave you stuck in a moment that you can't get out of.

You have to shake the fear and take the chance; otherwise, you'll miss out on something that may be life-changing.

Beyond feeling that initial fear, there is a lesson in rejection. Yes, it's not the outcome that anyone is looking for, but it's important to know it's not the be-all and end-all. It can be disheartening to have this happen, but you can't allow it to hinder your progress. Plus, the emotion isn't long-lasting. Moving past this may take some time, but it's completely possible to achieve this. It will be a process, but it's worth taking. We'll dive into this a bit more in a later chapter, so let's move forward.

Having shyness is something most men have, so it's not uncommon. Especially when engaging the opposite sex. It can be a daunting task and may bring out a little anxiety, but there are ways to steer the tide. Overcoming this obstacle won't be easy, as it's a trait that most of us possess in some fashion. However, there are ways to diagnose what's causing the shyness and finding ways to defeat or quell it.

Every person is shy, especially in the courtship stage. It's the fear of reaching out and finding someone new. This same feeling happens when making new friends as well. It's the fear of what they'll think of you, how you'll react to the meeting, and if you give off the impression intended. It's a lot of things to think about, which can give you anxiety on its own. The best thing to do is take things a step at a time. Trying to think of too much and all at once will cause you to second guess everything.

That's not to say that overcoming shyness is an easy feat. It may be one of the toughest traits to overcome. Some people have a natural ability to be open with anyone at any point, but it doesn't come so easy for most of us. This is one of those things that will require patience to overcome. You may need some time to work yourself up to starting the courtship or even a friendship.

Allow yourself this time, as it allows you to assess the situation. It's during this time you can self-reflect and use your strengths to help overcome your shyness. This could be something as simple as using your humor, your ability to talk, or finding something in common to break the ice. Any of these aspects will work in your favor.

In the end, it's finding that relatability, as we discussed before. Finding common ground will help build confidence and also help maintain the conversation. Continue to hone on these areas, and your confidence will continue to grow. Within this, you'll notice changes within the courtship and a possibility of further interest.

Other underlying issues can be anything that doesn't fall into the other categories. These can vary from something extremely small to a larger issue. While we can't break down all of the psychological aspects, we'll briefly touch those to the best of our abilities. We'll start with some of the smaller examples and determine ways to get over those humps.

If you're naturally a shy person, opening up can be extremely difficult. Meeting new people isn't your strong suit, and you'd much rather keep to yourself. These instances do occur as it is harder for some to branch out than others. Overcoming the fear of meeting new people is extremely hard but can be defeated. Feel out the person you're looking at courting just by mannerisms and signs.

This same aspect can be used for starting friendships. You can normally tell if people are warm to you through their actions. If you're a good reader of signs as opposed to talking, this is a huge advantage. Take this trait and use it to gauge if they're looking to pursue this further. It may end up being less awkward than stepping forward towards a losing cause.

If reading signs and talking aren't your strong traits, there are other ways to reach out. With technology being advanced, we now have the option to speak with someone without even being in the room. You can set the tone before even seeing a person. You can achieve this aspect by using dating sites or apps. There are plenty of these available on the internet and for all types of dating aspects.

If you're looking for a long-term relationship or even a small hook-up, there's a niche dating site available for you. You can use the website to tell your best story and reach

out without leaving your house! If you're more tech-savvy and are on the go, no problem! Apps also exist for the same reason and are more streamlined. The confidence you need could be right at your fingertips and could be just a profile match away.

Use the profile to build a strong character, highlighting your strengths. You can also use this profile to open up a bit about yourself, so those who may be interested know what you bring to the table. From there, if your profile matches another or catches someone's eye, you can communicate even further and start building that trust and chemistry. It's almost like a minor loophole for those who have trouble communicating in person.

Using this medium can also build your confidence tenfold, making the initial meet-up a lot smoother and less awkward. Use this to your advantage and put yourself out there! You have the options afforded to you to make yourself known without having to step fully out of your comfort zone. Of course, you'll still have to meet face to face, but having this in your back pocket will do wonders for the courtship and your confidence.

If there is a major psychological issue that may be preventing your confidence gain, then there's nothing wrong with reaching out for help. Seeking a professional to take care of your problems is one of the healthiest things you can do. It would be best if you didn't try to fix these problems solo, as that can lead to catastrophic and long-term effects. Not only affecting relationships and courtships but other aspects of life that you may not expect.

It's a better option to seek the help you need and get yourself together before attempting any pursuits, or at the very least, get a handle on your issues first. You may not be able to solve everything, and it will be a work in progress, but getting the steps together to get you in order shows your willingness to fix the issue.

Also, be wary of choosing the right treatment you will need. Knowing or having an idea of what's causing your confidence issues will require being open with them. Talk things out with your professional, so you're both on the same page, and be sure to pinpoint the issues that need to be resolved. There may be more than one, which is fine. As stated before, no one in life is perfect, but again, it's better to take that time and get the wheels turning than to try and figure things out on your own.

You can also use your time with the professional to build your other traits in courtship. Your relationship with your professional will require trust and communication, the very things you're looking to build in your romantic and platonic relationships. This partnership will require you to be open with someone else, something you're uncomfortable doing. Use the lessons learned and some of the aspects gained from this in your courtship or friendship stages. This will take time on both facets, but it will be more than worth it once settled.

Confidence is a trait that some have but can be gained with the right amount of work and patience on your part. You have to find your strengths through self-reflection, but also be humble with your findings. No one wants to be with anyone who's full of themselves, but don't downplay your abilities either. How you represent yourself is how others will see you, so always put your best foot forward.

If being completely open isn't your strong suit, find alternatives where you can show your strengths and put yourself out there. Dating apps and sites are a fine alternative to achieve this goal. Use your profile to express your strengths and to communicate before the initial face-to-face. Using this advantage will help build your confidence and reduce the anxiety that you may feel.

If you need more than just an alternative to gain that confidence, it never hurts to reach out. Making sure that you're okay is most important to confidence gain. Reach out to the proper professionals if need be and use what you've learned from their sessions to help in your process. Reaching out and seeking help will require you to be open with your emotions and feelings, but learning that here and trusting the professional to provide solutions is a step in the right direction.

Confidence can be tricky and something that takes time to build, but it's something we all have, and it just requires effort and time.

Chapter 4:

Take Your Time

In the previous chapters, we went over being relatable, gaining confidence to continue forging forward, and discovering your strengths while building that confidence. It's time to put it all together and see where things go. While doing so, you can't rush the situation. If you become too hasty and ask for too much and too soon, you may end up breaking up a relationship that you've put in the effort to build. As the old saying goes, Rome wasn't built in a day. Relationships take time and effort, and taking the right time is very important. This chapter will go over how to gauge the right time, use what's been learned so far, and determine when to take the next steps further.

The question is, how do you gauge the proper amount of time? The answer to that is, well, it depends. A big factor in gauging the amount of time is a judge of chemistry. You can have a ton in common and maybe maintain a conversation, but building chemistry is organic. The connection will move swimmingly if the chemistry is strong, almost like the time isn't moving. Keep in mind, however, that this trait won't happen overnight. It's going to require continuing to be relatable to your partner to keep it fostering.

These moments are where your active listening will need to go a bit further. You've used it to gather details, cues, and memories, but not we're looking for more relatable elements. Don't forget to continue engaging as well. Pace the conversation to a comfortable zone for both of you. In this instance, you'll need to follow their lead a bit. See how much they are willing to reveal and maintain the interest to reveal more to you. You'll begin to feel comfortable around one another, which will lead to further and deeper conversations.

We discussed those aspects of relatability in the first chapter. In building that chemistry, these will be equally important. Listening and looking for cues are going to help you in the matter. The more active listening you contribute, the better your chances of building that chemistry. It shows that you're listening and being attentive to your partner. Showing this ability will go a long way with building trust and understanding, which helps with chemistry.

As you continue to build that trust and chemistry, you'll begin to find similarities, differences, and some things you may not like. This process is common when going through the courtship stage. No matter how perfect we'd like to build someone up, there will be cons to them as well. It's during these conversations and moments where time will be of utmost importance. The main goal of all of this is to find someone as a lifelong partner, so you'll have to manage their good traits with their bad ones. Are the traits that they have bad enough to sway you from continuing? Are there any bad habits they may have that would cause this courtship to end abruptly?

Weighing these pros and cons is important for the long-term stability of the relationship. Keep in mind, while you're evaluating theirs, your faults will be looked into by them as well. Per the last chapter, we determined what your strengths were and when to use them. In the early courtship stage, it's easy for those to shine through at first, but eventually, the newness will wear off, and some of the faults in your character will begin to show. Any bad habits you may have will also be seen and put under a microscope. You have to determine, at this point, what you're willing to work on or if there are any traits you're willing to give up.

The pros and cons stage sounds exhausting and stressful, but it doesn't necessarily have to be. This reason is why active listening and engagement are so important. You learn these things about yourself and your partner through communication and listening. Maybe you didn't notice something in the early stages, but you see it now. Is it something you can look past? Is it a string trait? Is it something you don't want to be around?

You'll learn this and so much more through active communication. It's a building block to gaining that relatability. Besides, if the chemistry is strong enough, these cons will seem small in the long run or even as a cute little quirk. Either way, you're building that trust and chemistry, which adds to being relatable. You'll even touch on topics that you may not know much about but are important to your partner. Even if it's a topic that you don't share, that makes it more important.

Sharing knowledge is a lot like sharing precious memories and moments. It goes with the openness and trust that you're looking to build. Again, chemistry is more of an organic situation, but showing an active interest in your partner's hobbies or activities will go long. Having this aspect in hand will also allow you to open up more to them, which can help build your confidence and chemistry.

If you're being introduced to a hobby or topic that your partner finds interesting, that's is more than just gaining some new insight. It's an instance of shared trust and understanding. Most people aren't willing to share a lot about themselves, let alone something they find near and dear to them.

Some people are even ashamed to reveal such things in part of how people will view them for enjoying such a guilty pleasure or having that "useless knowledge." The trust is that you won't judge them for their interests or activities. You don't necessarily have to join them, but still support their endeavors as you would your own. They don't need someone else looking down on them for enjoying themselves.

Now, this also isn't to say that you don't have your boundaries either. If you don't feel comfortable with it or it's an activity you can't support, you have the right not to. Please don't make a scene of it and don't degrade the person, but stand your ground in a friendly but firm manner. Judgment still shouldn't be used in this type of situation as it will make things even more awkward, but do what you can to remove yourself from the situation if need be.

You can be a little selfish in this stage as, again, you're looking for a lifelong partner in the end. Don't reduce your comfort level to the point that you forget about yourself. Know your limits and boundaries. Relationships are a give and take, and you don't want to give too much.

In the same vein of pros and cons, activities and interests are also ranked similarly. There will be some things you're into that your potential partner either may not know or may not approve of. It's up to you and how you feel the trust factor is in the relationship to relay this knowledge to her, then gauge her interest. If she's given enough of herself to you in the engagement stage, you owe it to the relationship to return the favor.

Much in the same way that you shouldn't sacrifice all of yourself for her, she has that same right. She will also have a comfort level that she may bend for you, but she won't break it. If you have an interest that she's not keen on, she will let you know of this. It's at this point that you have to decide if the interest is worth it. Are you willing to give this up for the good of the relationship? Is this activity or interest that important that you're willing to risk your partner?

From there, it's up to you to decide how important this activity is to you and your relationship. If she's worth the sacrifice, then make it for the sake of the relationship. You'll find that she'll do the same for you on something you may not like. If it's something you can't drop immediately, then show steps of removing it from your life. She'll support you in your endeavor as she knows you're making the change for her.

This change shows a bit of exchanged chemistry and trust and shows maturity in a sense. You're willing to move on from something to move forward with a new venture. You trust her enough to change a small bit of yourself to be with her. Most individuals wouldn't do this as they can be more selfish than most in a relationship, but you made that sacrifice. This instance makes you stand out in her eyes and can lead things to progress further.

Providing the proper emotion in situations also is a thing with time. You don't want to rush into an awkward situation immediately. This aspect can stunt the growth of the relationship or end it. This is where looking at cues will be important, and we'll look at some that could help in going down the right path.

Certain instances, done by individuals in the courtship stage, can be taken out of context while communicating. Something may have been said that was meant one way but taken the complete opposite. We're all prone to it, and it happens more often than you think. Especially if you're an individual who communicates through text first, it's hard to read emotion through a set of words, so knowing cues and reading tones is very important.

It's during these times that you need to figure out how to handle your emotions. If you're on the side of the offended, don't immediately lose yourself in the misunderstanding. Ask your partner what they meant by the statement. Getting clarity on a situation is much better than jumping to conclusions. Not to mention that doing so shows insecurity, which is a trait that many are turned off by.

On the opposite side, if you inadvertently made the offense, gauge the situation. See how your partner is feeling about what was said and clarify accordingly. Understand why the offense was taken and calmly explain what you truly meant by what was stated. Also, understand that this may not absolve of you any wrongdoing, and it may take time for them to forgive. You'll have to allow them that time as they would give you the same courtesy.

There may also be instances where skirmishes may occur. Not necessarily anything that would lead to a break-up, but a minor fight where cooler heads didn't prevail. No courtship is perfect,

and these emotions will arise. What's important is how you handle yourself and your partner in these times. There will be hurt feelings and possible days of no contact. You'll have to let these ride for a little while to heal from the fight, especially if it's the first one.

You don't expect to have any issues with a new partner, but they will happen. Are you going to roll with the punches of the new relationship, or does the buck stop here? How you handle this instance emotionally will take a toll on how things go from here. Don't allow yourself to get overzealous in these moments. Keep your cool, let things simmer down, then reach out the olive branch.

Being in tune with your emotions and hers is another sign of well-built chemistry, but it will also take time and trials to get it right. These things can't be rushed and left to emotion. You have to sit back and look at the full picture and communicate once it's time to do so. That communication after a fight is important as it will help put things back on the right track to continue forward in the courtship.

Though holding a conversation isn't the only important thing to chemistry, it doesn't mean it isn't helpful. Holding down and continuing a conversation is a trait that can add to the bond portion of chemistry. You can also pick up more cues from this aspect. Some of them will be specific if you know what to look for or recognize the conversation's tone.

Though this has been stressed often, active listening will help determine the tone and vibe. This aspect helps beyond the get to know you stage, but also in small talk and space-filling. Every conversation you have with your partner won't be completely thought-provoking or memorable. There will be times where you will need to fill that void. How you do so depends on how you engage the conversation and listen for cues to see if the conversation is worth continuing. Your partner will also attempt this on occasion.

Be active in these moments and join her in the activity. Dead space, especially early in the relationship, can be a sign of boredom and disinterest. You have to stay on top of your communication, or you may see yourself remaining alone. You can't entertain your partner as you would yourself. You may have to step outside your comfort a little bit to usher things along.

There may be instances where silence is golden, though, and you have to be aware of those. Some individuals want to vibe with you while doing their own thing. There doesn't necessarily have to be any talking, and it could just be minor cues and mannerisms. It's the trust and love of having that person in the room with them that they enjoy. Enjoying someone's company while enjoying your activities and interests is another huge sign of chemistry and trust. It shows that you don't have to keep that person's attention all the time, but you have it when you need it. You're allowing them to be themselves and in their moment while being with you.

It's a nonverbal communication cue that does wonders in most relationships. The best thing is you'll receive this same courtesy from your partner. They'll offer you your space while you enjoy your activities but still share the room with you. It's another instance where your chemistry and trust are at an all-time high, and the relatability is off the charts.

Using those aspects mentioned above, we can determine the next steps that need to be taken to progress. It's all about looking at what we've discovered so far and building to achieve progression in the courtship.

Time is needed to build chemistry and trust to maintain the proper relationship. If you attempt to rush these moments, it can only lead to disaster in the end, and no one wants to have that kind of situation. Through proper communication, active listening, and knowing your emotions, you can maneuver through all obstacles that stand in your path. It's up to you and your partner to build these things together to achieve the outcome you're looking for.

When active listening, go deep than just the get to know you stage. At this point, you are past that, and you'll have to put in the time to learn more about their quirks, activities, and even small talk. You'll also find things you may not like about your partner, and you'll have to determine if putting in that time is worth it. You and your partner's patience in the relationship be tested, and it's up to you both to decide what aspects are worth keeping and which are worth sacrificing. You'll need to communicate openly and over time to determine if the relationship is worth continuing.

You're going to learn many new things about your partner, and they may even share activities and interests with you that they've never shared with anyone. Keep in tune with this as it shows trust. You don't necessarily have to join in or enjoy the same things, but show support if it's constructive and doesn't hurt anyone. Adding that support from you goes a long way to building that chemistry in the relationship, and they'll trust you to be more open with you.

Furthermore, they'll show the same respect for your interests and activities. Having this give and take provides another milestone in the progression of the courtship and adds to the trust and understanding you need to proceed.

Just as important as small and filling the void, having those nonverbal communication skills are also fruitful. Though initially, having a dead air, nonspeaking type of hang out may seem like a sign of disinterest, those times will become more of a pleasant experience as you two get closer. You're both are allowed to be in your own element while being together. Yes, communication through a relationship is very important, and talking with your partner is needed.

However, some days you want to chill, vibe, and hang out while doing your own thing. This achievement is at an all-time high when it comes to trust and chemistry. You're both able to vibe nonverbally and maintain each other's interests simultaneously.

Putting in that time to achieve these moments will only prove to be beneficial for the relationship's health. As stated before, you can't rush these moments, and you have to put in the work and time to get to this point. These moments will be some of the most important to achieve the end goal of a lasting relationship. Hold these moments sacred, and don't put any rush into them. Doing this and maintaining yourself will build your confidence as well.

Time and patience are virtues, especially in relationship building. Most people last to rush through things and try to get to the end of the race. A relationship can't be treated as such, as it's more of a marathon. If you try to sprint through your courtship and force things that aren't ready, you'll end up hurting yourself, losing your partner, and ending something you've worked so hard for. Take your time, pace yourself, and you'll see the fruits of your labor grow. Now, all you have to do is wait for the fruits to be ripe for the picking. In time, you'll realize that the juice will be well worth the squeeze and the wait.

Chapter 5:

Follow Her Lead

In the courtship stage, a lot of men tend to try and take the lead. Sometimes this can work in your favor and can be fruitful, but in several other cases, it's better to "look at her shoes," so to speak. In essence, sometimes, she should take the lead.

Now, this shoe philosophy can be taken metaphorically and literally. By this, I mean taking a look at her shoes instead of her eyes. As we are mainly attracted to the eyes, she may already see what she needs to and possibly has already moved on. However, paying attention to her shoes means you are attentive to detail. She'll feel the choice was an intended attention getter and be more astute to your movements. It's a form of allowing her to take the lead.

We feel that we have to take over every detail in the dating phase in most cases. We like to dictate the pace and try to forge our own path to the result without considering the person we're pursuing, especially if things appear to run smoothly through the courtship. We don't take the time to pay attention to small things and instead shoot for the big goal. This lack of attention to detail will prove to backfire if this path continues. Not taking into account what your partner wants to achieve in this courtship leads to many misconceptions and misunderstandings. That's why it's equally as important to relinquish the lead.

For example, within the initial dating stage, we may focus on physical appearance. This process isn't bad by any means, but it's more or less about what we look for. Many men falter in this stage because we look at the purely physical and not why they made that fashion or style decision. We don't draw attention to the details. Maybe she wore her hair a certain way, wore the dress for a certain reason, has on jewelry for a specific occasion. Sure, we may notice these things and compliment them, but we don't take the time to determine their reasoning. Women pick up on this and will make a snap decision based on your reactions.

If the reaction is what she's looking for, she will continue the pursuit along with you. She'll even be more intrigued by you because you noticed these small cues. If the reaction is a non-reaction or contrary to what she wants, consider this a game-over moment. By this time, she knows you're not paying full attention to her and what she's doing. She'll look at this as complacency and, though she may continue the date, her decision to no longer pursue has already happened. All of this has gone on in a matter of seconds, and you may not even know that it transpired.

These moments of following her lead will also require your active listening to be on a high. We've discussed the importance of active listening through the first few chapters, but in following her lead, it's come out tenfold. You're attempting to pick up on all the small instances and focusing on them. Even something as small as her shoes. Now, that doesn't mean to interrogate her on every piece of clothing she has on, but to show that you've noticed changes will work wonderfully in your favor.

For example, if you've been hanging out for a while, and the dress has been pretty casual on her part, but this particular night she requests a bit of a dressier occasion, pick up on that. This aspect is part of her taking the lead in the courtship stage and showing she wants to progress further. Again, you don't need to ask why this request is happening, but address the situation and follow the lead accordingly.

Be sure to put your best foot forward in this instance. Take the request seriously and show up at your into the date as much as she is. You don't need to overshadow her but match the level she's on or looking for. Showing up unprepared or underdressed may seem like you're disinterested in the entire situation. This date has a bit more stakes as she wants to step things up and move forward. Not stepping up to the challenge will be detrimental to the courtship.

On the other side, this small gesture will make her see you in a positive light. It shows that you take her suggestions to heart and view her as an equal. You're not trying to strong-arm the courtship and make it your own but build it with both of your images while still maintaining the goal. It also shows a bit of a maturity level. Not just because you're willing to dress up on occasion, but that you're willing to step out of your comfort zone for her. You're in tune with her progression and paying attention to the details, even the small ones.

These smaller details will also become significant, as they will show her being comfortable with you. Again, these will be instances of her taking the lead. If the relationship is going well, she may begin to initiate contact and visitation. Most men would be taken back by this as they feel they should dictate when and where any dates or meet-ups should occur. Don't draw yourself back from this; allow her to take the lead. This instance shows that you trust her instincts and style. This also shows that you're willing to be spontaneous, which adds freshness to the courtship.

Beyond this, and most importantly, it builds a trust element. Allowing her to run the date, pick the spots, and maintain the pace, will throw her into the lead position. You trust her and what she can bring to the table. You want to build more chemistry by seeing what she's into and allowing for her to maintain control of the date. You're allowing her to take the lead, and she will acknowledge this, wanting to show you the best time possible. Keep in mind; she'll also want your feedback on the date and how you're enjoying yourself. This aspect is part of the process.

In following her lead, she wants the assurance that things are still going well. It's not a self-conscious type of reason but for compatibility. If you aren't enjoying yourself on the date she chose, it's an instant step backward. If you're enjoying yourself, say so and show that her lead is taken seriously and sincerely.

Engage in the date and continue to show interest, but don't overdo it. You don't want to seem disingenuous, but you want to be intrigued. Don't feign interest, as it will be noticeable. If you can't be honest about this instance, then that shows an instant reg flag on your part. Not to mention the effect on the overall chemistry, as she'll question past instances and things done.

In the same vein, if the date doesn't interest you, then do say so. Now, this isn't the answer she would be looking for, but it shows your honesty. It goes back to feigning interest and how easily it's read. Women pick up on cues faster than us and will immediately see your tells. If you're not enjoying yourself and lying about it, the trust factor is shattered, and the courtship is over. An important pillar broke on the smallest of lies, but still significant. Being honest from the beginning is more beneficial in the long run.

With that said, you don't need to be brutally honest. Inform her that it's not your ideal dating situation, but you're willing to continue. It's not rude to state that this isn't your cup of tea. Don't ridicule her for her date choice, and be as respectful as possible when stating your dislike. She may not enjoy your reaction to her choice, but she would respect how you handled the situation. It shows maturity in a situation that most may not have a level head. Keep in mind; there's another way to work around this aspect. If you show that you enjoy her company while being in an uncomfortable situation, it'll go a long way to help you too.

It's not the best scenario, but it occurs. You can still enjoy being on a bad date if you enjoy the company that's with you. This aspect can happen at any stage, but we're using the following her lead example. You can still enjoy her company even if you don't enjoy her date selection. It may change your mind about the selection itself. You'll hold the memory of the "bad date" but having a good time with your partner. Through following her lead, you were able to see a positive in something you didn't like before and create a memory that both of you will cherish.

There are other instances where following her lead will be a part of the courtship process, mainly through watching her movements and mannerisms. Keeping abreast of these minor details may lead you further progress in the courtship then you originally thought. One instance is in public displays of affection. Most men tend to rush the PDA in a courtship. We want to go for certain movements, such as kisses or deep hugs, a lot sooner than their potential partner would like. With PDA, you want to take it a bit slower and follow her lead.

You don't want to rush showing affection, as this may lead to many misunderstandings. Women have their own set of rules for showing affection, and many would rather dictate the time and place for said showings. If you bullrush into a kiss, it will lead to an awkward moment, especially if she's not ready.

Before jump to a conclusion, read the room and see where things are. You'll want to follow her lead when it comes to the context clues. Be aware of small instances and what she will allow.

If she wants you to hold her hand, she'll offer it. If she wants a deep hug, she'll pull you in closer. If she wants to offer a kiss, she'll meet you halfway. Forcing yourself into the situation will immediately end a courtship. Not to mention it will crush any chemistry and trust you may have built up. You don't want this ending, so avoid it at all costs.

It's always important to keep in mind that you don't have to dictate everything regarding the courtship. Yes, we like to maintain control of the courtship stage in an attempt to get to the goal we're looking for. However, it's just as important to consider your partner's role and how much they can dictate the pace. Following her lead in many instances can lead to new things learned about her as well as yourself. Not to mention building more trust and relatability as well as chemistry in the courtship.

If you want to follow her lead effectively, you will need to be in tune with the details she provides. Notice the changes that she makes or the requests that she gives. Lean into these requests and cues and respond as needed. This doesn't mean that you feign any interest or try to hide true feelings, be honest. She'll respect your honesty and feedback on the situation more than the false interest shows. She'll also be able to read if you're not genuine.

You'll also want to follow her lead with public displays of affection. Trying to rush these instances will lead to awkward moments and misunderstandings. It's important to read cues and understand tones. You don't want to go for too much too soon, and your partner will shut you down quickly if you can't read the cues correctly. Paying attention to these details will work in your favor and lead to higher favorability.

This all starts with "looking at her shoes." Putting yourself in the back seat and following her footsteps in the courtship. It may sound uneasy, but looking for the right elements in the right moments will help move the courtship along.

Chapter 6:

Accept and Learn From Rejection

In following her lead, you may end up at a small fork in the road. It's either the path lined with the goal in mind of a relationship or the realization that maybe things aren't going to work out. Such is life, in most instances, and these outcomes are normally no fault of either party. Just sometimes, things don't go the way you'd like. Rejection is hard; that goes without saying. However, this isn't the end of the world for you. Just because things didn't work out on this particular instance doesn't mean it can't be elsewhere. Also, keep in mind, you will gain knowledge and a little something extra in the end. This chapter will go over how to deal with the possibility of rejection and what lessons to take away from the situation.

The first thing that needs to be realized is that this isn't the end of the world. At the moment, it may feel like one of the worst felt pains because of the newness, but this feeling will pass. With that said, this doesn't mean to disregard how you're feeling completely. It's okay to feel the vulnerability of the loss and to allow yourself to heal. The healing process will be where you'll learn most about yourself and continue the growth needed. The issue is harboring those feelings and using that to try and move forward.

Before going to the self-reflection phase, there is dealing with the emotions of the breakup. The feeling of rejection is not fun in any aspect, let alone when looking for a partner. It hurts when things don't work out or plan, and it's easy to go to a dark place because of it. Keep in mind that it's okay to have these feelings. You have to allow yourself to hurt to heal. Not allowing yourself to do so and putting yourself right back on the saddle could prove to hurt you again.

Getting in on the rebound game only allows for momentary gratification. You're not doing this because you're looking for another courtship; you're doing this to get over the previous one. It shows the hurt you're still going through but using someone else to get over it. Now, instead of fixing yourself, you've burned two bridges and put yourself right back at square one. Take the time you need to get over the heartache, but do so in healthy and constructive ways. Using another person to do so shows the power that person had over you and the maturity still needed by you to hold a courtship. You can't fight fire with a bigger fire; then everyone gets burned.

You also can't allow the rejection of the past to affect your present. A major problem from a breakup, good or bad, is that many of us will maintain generalizations from it. Every girl does this or does that, which paints future courtships in a negative light. If you begin to generalize all courtship opportunities, you'll miss out on more than you'll expect. No one wants to be with a person who will constantly compare them to a previous encounter. You have to look at each one as a clean slate and move on accordingly. Hanging on to the past is another instance of not truly assessing your feelings and moving forward. You'll find out quickly that you'll remain by yourself if you continue to live in the past.

Learning from this rejection is also accepting that things didn't work out. Some people will try and force a situation again, thinking that things will go differently if tried from a different aspect. Though this can happen, it's normally not for the best and can lead to further separation. If things didn't work out the first, it's best to let the past be the past. If the partner is truly that important, then they will come back to you. Chasing after past pursuits leaves you stagnant, plus can keep you from exploring options you may not have noticed. While chasing someone from your past, you could be missing signs to better your future.

Allowing this individual moment to dictate the remainder of your relationships will stunt your growth as a person. It will also make it harder for future courtships and possible friendships you're looking to forge. You never want to rest on unhappiness, no matter how you feel at the time. It's in these moments that you look into yourself and see if maybe there were things that could've gone differently.

After assessing your feelings and thoughts, we move into self-reflection. We've mentioned this process in the gaining confidence section, but it's just as important when dealing with rejection. There could be many underlying reasons why things didn't work out, but it's just as important to know what could've been changed from your perspective. Maybe a trait you initially saw as a positive became a negative. Maybe there was an instance of being too hasty and reading too much into a situation. Maybe the chemistry wasn't as strong as it was initially. How did these things happen, and what could be done differently in the future? It's these examples of questions that you can ask to help lead to your solution.

While determining these factors, it's also important to determine what is salvageable. By this, I mean finding the shortcoming that happened and building upon it. It doesn't necessarily mean you came on too strong or used this trait too much, but maybe you didn't use it enough. If you're a talkative person but couldn't keep a conversation, determine why this happened. What caused you to close down when you were open before? Was it a gut feeling you felt after the initial contact or something else underlying? What can I do from here to build upon this trait to maintain it through the relationship?

This reflection on yourself will help you answer some of your questions. Of course, with rejection, you're going to have more questions that you can't answer alone. This answer will require a bit more effort on your part if you're looking for that closure. Some answers may be left unanswered, but the curiosity of what happened will linger. This also is determined by how things fell apart. If things ended amicably, there's a possibility to gain that closure.

Depending on how things fell apart, you could always speak with the partner in question. If it ended on positive terms, your partner might be more willing to talk things out and explained what truly went wrong. That's part of why, even in rejection, try to maintain some positivity out of it if possible.

Understandably, this isn't easy in many cases, but sometimes it can prove to work favorably. It could've been a misunderstanding that could be fixed or anything with those lines. If closure is needed, then this communication will be important. You never want to rest on just one side of the story if you can conclude civilly.

Get a good feel as to what happened and why things didn't work out to fruition. From this talk, you can learn if there are any shortcomings you may have missed, cues you didn't pick up on, or if the chemistry itself just wasn't there. It could be an instance where the strong traits make you a good friend to them, but not necessarily what they are looking for in a partner. It doesn't mean there's anything wrong with you personally.

That means you're still a person they're willing to talk, hang, and express themselves freely. They still want you in their life in some capacity, which still strikes a great deal of importance. This information is useful for building future courtships and relationships.

For example, maybe things didn't work out between you two, but maybe she has a friend that may be more compatible. If you two maintain a positive companionship, there's a possibility of a future courtship down the road. It may not have been who you were after initially, but it may lead to something better for you. The former partner becomes a friend and will look out for you as such. Though it isn't a relationship based on courtship anymore, it's still an important relationship worth keeping.

It may seem like a bad deal to forge a friendship with a failed courtship partner, but it's less stressful in the end. You find that you relate to someone who shares similar thoughts and goals and would work better as a platonic life partner than a betrothed couple. It may not have been the bond you were looking for at first, but a new one blossomed for a situation that could've been awkward. Furthermore, burning this bridge could lead to more damage than you were expecting and added stress to an already bad situation.

That's not to say those bad fallouts won't happen. One of the terrible truths to breakups or failed courtships is they don't always end amicably. This bad ending can happen for several reasons, but the most important thing is not to allow it to consume you. People will call each other the bad guy in all breakups. Depending on the story you hear, it's a different situation each time. The best way to handle these types of breakups is to not feed into any rumors or lies. You know what happened in the relationship, so it should stay that way. Entertaining hearsay only leaves you to ridicule, and in some instances, can prove the hearsay right. Stay your course and continue to move forward.

You also can't allow this deeply negative instance to affect your other potential suitors. This is one common mistake that most of us make. We tend to take negative traits learned from previous courtships and apply them to new ones. Or we rely on past generalizations to justify why we aren't in a courtship now.

These thoughts are counterproductive to the whole task of mingling. Applying and generalizing leads to missed opportunities, and there's no sense in doing so. You're only harming yourself by holding on to these emotions.

The stress alone of holding onto these feelings can also be very taxing. They'll take a toll on your confidence as you'll be plagued with self-doubt. These thoughts will filter into every little social engagement from there and forward. There will be fear of running into one another, scenes possibly made, or the awkward moments of being stuck together and an unwanted setting. That anxiety will permeate into every other situation, and you'll be stuck either looking over your shoulder or not going out at all.

If there were other underlying issues, again, it's not the end of the world for you. To err is human, and we're all susceptible to our shortcomings. There are ways to internalize this information and use it to progress yourself further and put yourself back out there. We'll go over a few things to consider during this time of reflection and ways to help mend the issues to move forward.

Just like with shyness, underlying issues can be a variety of different things. Just know that there is always help for you in these instances. If going through the self-reflection stage doesn't help you get to the answers you need and asking the significant other doesn't help or isn't an option, there's another place you can turn to.

Your friends can help you find the underlying issues by being an outside perspective. If your bond and trust are strong with them, they will offer advice and tips based on their relationship with you. They'll be comfortable enough to get you the constructive criticism needed without being too harsh or abrasive. Trust these critiques, even if they cut a little deep.

These takes are filled with honesty and love. It may be a little tough, but real friends will offer these to you to help better yourself. This reason is why forming bonds of all types is extremely important, not just in courtship. They'll help provide more building blocks to elevate yourself and raise your confidence. We'll discuss these aspects further in a later chapter.

If the issues are beyond talking and require more insight, always know that professionals can help you through your plight. Just like with confidence and shyness, some reason as to why you can't overcome the phobia may be psychological. Remember that asking for help, even from a professional, is not a sign of failure or weakness.

It takes a strong person to understand that they can't do certain things independently and that asking their inner circle doesn't solve things. Digging deeper into your issues and making an attempt to solve them is the best practice to take. Working with this aspect may even help with the self-reflection and taking criticism stages. It allows a third party to take personal feelings out of their diagnosis and examine the problem with clearer eyes.

From there, pinpoints and habits for these issues are found, and ways to fix them are established. Either through sessions of talking things or a need for alternative means is necessary; getting these fixed will go a long way to mending the fences needed to establish stronger bonds and relationships. Never think you have to battle this alone, as there are ways to get through your issues. Those ways will require admitting to the issues you have, which will require humility on your part. Keep in mind, however, that having this humility is another sign of strength for yourself. All of this is a step in the right direction to making yourself a better you and further learn from this setback.

Rejection is painful and will be a process to deal with. How you handle the rejection is completely up to you. We know there are negative ways to handle the loss, which must be avoided at all costs. Not doing so will only hurt you and will bleed into other aspects of your social engagements. Harboring these negative feelings also leads to generalizations that will damage other attempted courtships. To move on, you can't hold on to this extra baggage. You have to let it go and allow that moment to stay in the past.

Going on rebounds also shows that you're still holding on to that weight. Though it can lead to a minor confidence boost, in the end, it's only a temporary high. Not to mention, you've now affected another person in the situation instead of handling it personally. The rebound road will add stress to an already awkward situation and doesn't address the issue at hand. It's a small bandaid on a massive wound that needs time to heal. Give yourself that time and allows those emotions to subside.

Once you've established this, self-reflect on the courtship. Look at the situation from a new set of eyes and focus on what may have lead to the ending. There may have been areas where your traits played too strongly, not enough, or the chemistry just wasn't right for the moment. Also, know that sometimes these things happen and not to take them too seriously. You can always move, and it may even be to something better down the road.

If you can avoid it, try not to end on adverse terms. Miscommunications can happen, and you never know what other bond may form from the courtship. Sure, things didn't end in a relationship, but that doesn't mean completely doing away with the person. You are still connected in some way, and those traits may work better in a platonic friendship. They're still a part of your life, just in a different aspect. Don't look at it as a failed courtship but as a found friendship. Plus, this may open other doors that you didn't know existed prior.

If adversity is unavoidable, then don't feed into the drama. Added stress to an already bad situation reflects terribly on you and can affect your future social engagements. Know your side and move on, but don't stoop to continuing a war of hurt feelings. Fighting fire with another fire only spreads the damage, and there's no need to scorch the Earth any further. Doing this is another sign of not letting things go and will only eat at you in the end.

Look to your friends to also help you in this time of need. They will offer constructive criticism to help pinpoint the issues you may have had. They will also be honest with you about your shortcomings and offers alternatives to help mend those habits. These moments are when strong bonds are needed with those friends as they'll be firm yet fair. It's also in these times when you know which friends have your best interests at heart. Take what they say and keep it with you. They can help in the lesson and be the rock you need while you heal from the crash.

Seek the professionals needed to help with your lesson if you need to. Rejection can be hard to handle alone, and friends may not have all the answers you're looking for. Show the humility needed to get the help you seek as well. Don't look at this moment as a sign of weakness. We all have issues that may require more resources than we expected. Use them to your advantage and get the help you need, and don't be ashamed to do so.

You'll live through the rejection, as it's not the end of the world. Not holding the courtship also doesn't make you a failure, as we've all been through it. It's all about how you handle yourself, use your resources, and learn from the situation. Taking a lesson from what's considered defeat is going to help you grow in the long run. It'll also be beneficial for you to be a better person for yourself and the next time you get on the dating saddle. You can't allow this rejection to plague you or leave you down. There are other fish out there in the sea. Just reel that hook in and cast out again when you're ready.

Chapter 7:

Bonding and Friendship

Beyond being a courtship or relationship, there's a couple of other aspects to consider. The ability to build a bond and form friendships are equally as important. These aspects are realized when a physical relationship with the courted partner may not be formed, or there's too much other noise affecting the flow of the relationship.

Having friends and forming bonds can help in the reduction of this aspect. Sometimes you will need some time away from the relationship or rely on someone to help mend after a failed courtship. That's why forming bonds and creating friends will be of great importance. These friends will be the ones you turn to for that release from reality or the break from the courtship. You'll also look to these individuals for possible tips and hints should you need them.

Bonding and friendships will save you during the low periods, especially during times of heartache. It's these moments where having friends can be very uplifting. They'll be your shoulder to cry on in your darkest moments and understand where your feelings are. They'll meet you on your level and attempt to help you build yourself back to the person you were before the break-up. If you need additional help, these friends will help lead you in the right direction and won't ridicule or talk down to you as you're healing. These are the types of reinforcement needed, and a strong bond and friendship with those around you will bring that together.

Before you can have friends like these, you have to know how to and what to look for. There is an approach you can try of trying to friend everyone that walks in front of you. There's nothing wrong with being this open and inclusive, and it could lead to a rather large circle. However, these won't be friends but mere acquaintances that's you met along the way. There are no real bonds shared or trust built, but you know who these people are. You're going to have to do much more than just putting yourself out there to build these traits and form these relationships.

There are several ways to achieve true friendship and bonding, but it will require you to court. It sounds similar to finding a life partner, and in many ways, it is. When you're creating a friendship with someone, you're looking at it lasting for an extended period. You don't want friends that are only along for a short while. Beyond building a friendship, you're looking to establish a bond—something beyond just being an acquaintance and brief conversation. You want to build something stronger with this individual and forge a long-lasting and fruitful platonic relationship.

It sounds like a daunting task, almost anxiety driving. It'll be a process to find those types of people to build these bonds with. You have to consider that this person, or people, is someone you're looking to share a bit of yourself with and grow together. Again, you're not looking to have a large circle of people you know, but long-lasting friendships. It's close to the other aspects of courtship we spoke about previously.

Though it sounds similar when building a relationship, courting for a friend does have a few differences. There may be traits you'd look for in a friend that you wouldn't necessarily want in a partner. For example, you may want a more subdued partner but a friend who is the life of the party. This reason may be because you require different tastes or want different dynamics for different situations. If it's a friendly environment, you may want to be with a friend that's more lively and able to grab the room's attention. Whereas in a relationship, you may want to be more intimate and calm, so a more subdued individual works better.

You have to know which type of person you are to know who you will vibe best with on a friendship level. Knowing this determines if you're either introverted or extroverted. The difference is how you express yourself and your personality. If you're a person who works better in smaller groups and is more reversed, you're an introverted person. If you have more expressive and more boisterous, you're an extroverted person. You can also have traits of both instances, which is called an omnivert. Communication skills are another primary difference between these types.

Communication is still key, even in forming friendships. Depending on how close you would like the bond to be, what you choose to share is up to you. If you're looking for a close bond in a friendship, you must be more of an open book. This is where knowing your introvert or extrovert traits will be key in how you will communicate. Each one communicates entirely differently, and knowing who you are will prove to be important.

Being introverted in the friendship stage is workable but makes courting difficult, and maintaining those friends is almost impossible. If you have the introverted trait, it's best to have friends that don't require a lot of maintenance. This way, it allows you to hang out on the more stagnant turns without feeling like it's an obligation each time. It's not a friendship you have to devote a mass amount of time and energy to, but one that will last as it's still maintainable.

Having friends that are in your comfort zone is beneficial as these bonds will be easier to manage. Introverts tend to hang with other introverts because of this. As such, you tend to share similar interests and activities, making bonding easier in the long run. These friends will be with you for the long haul. They know what you offer and can offer the same in return because you share the same traits. You may not communicate often, but when you do, it's like no time is lost. You pick things up from where they left off, and there's no awkwardness due to time.

You're also more willing to be open with a person of a similar trait. This aspect is mainly due to the initial trust of that person.

If you click with or share a personality type, it's easy to be more open and honest with that person. You know how to open up with one another because you share a similar trait. Beyond that, you know each other's boundaries and the time needed to achieve that larger understanding. You don't throw everything out at once, and each of you gauges each other's perspectives because you can understand them.

Keep in mind that even with two introverts who understand each other, the courtship stage will still be difficult. Most introverts keep their guard up and don't like to show their full hand. There will be a feeling-out process between the both of you. This process is also a trust type of situation.

It boils down to who will reveal more or who's willing to reveal more. You want to build trust amongst each other but are still hesitant to do so. This reason could be due to past instances, general feelings, or the anxiety of meeting someone new. Either way, you want the same result, but it still may be difficult to get there because of the nature of the trait.

If you are more of an extrovert, achieving a stronger bond and finding like-minded people will be the goal. This makes courting easier for all parties involved as there is no need to reel yourself in. Extroverts tend to be freer, and hanging with those that have that same feeling will add to that aspect for yourself.

Just like with two introverts, two extroverts may be drawn to each other quicker due to similarities. They like to be lives of the party and will gravitate immediately to others like them. This makes pointing their type out in a crowd simple and easy to come together when needed. Because of this, clicking together becomes easy, and you're more open to express yourself. The trait similarities allow you to feel each other out, but the courting process goes quicker. Conversation can bounce from small talk to deep thoughts because extroverts can communicate on a dime.

Being open and honest with each other isn't hard because you can communicate your feelings and build trust easier as an extrovert. This also may lead to chemistry as friends being built quicker because of the open dialogue. The problem is if the dialogue is genuine. Extroverts can use various emotions to hide their true feelings at that given time. Even though you may have clicked in the initial meeting, it may have been all for not as the person you're clicking with wasn't genuine with their feelings toward you. They knew they could click with you and used that for their own comfort.

For extroverts, it boils down to who's genuine with the other. It's a similar situation to introverts as it's a mechanism to keep your guard up. It could be for similar reasons as introverts as well. Though it's easier to go through the courtship stage, it's still a feeling-out process.

There's a bit of a chess game of the give and take. Yes, both are openly communicating, but it starts mostly with generalized small talk. Once that fades, from there, it's wondering if this person is willing to share as much as you do. You may toss out small tidbits of yourself to see if they bite and find more of a common ground outside of what's been said.

As we discussed before, an extrovert and introvert friendship are difficult to come by, but some of the most fruitful relationships come from this category. An old saying says opposites attract, and this is the case that two polar opposites will join together. An extrovert and an introvert can form a strong bond and friendship because they compliment each other for as opposite as they are. An extrovert can help an introvert break out of their shell and open up a bit more, while an introvert can help an extrovert be a bit more subdued when needed. They are essential the yen to each other's yang. That perfect balance for one another that will help each other grow as individuals and friends.

Once you've determined your type and see which individuals you vibe with the most, you begin to build that chemistry between you two. This is handled through communication, which goes from small talk to deeper conversations; this is when the bond is formed. You find common topics, aspects, goals, and thoughts that you share and discuss.

Through this bonding stage, you'll both be comfortable with one another to open up and be vulnerable. This process is the true test of trust that will weigh heavy on this friendship. The more you open up and give of yourself, the higher the trust will be in the friendship—the more trust in the friendship, the stronger the bond.

You want to be an open book to those you want these long-lasting friendships with. Be as open as you possibly can, and your friendship partner will reciprocate. They want to be there for you as much as they can, and if you give them ample reasoning, they will provide that structure. In the same vein, you also need to be in tune with their side of the platonic courtship.

In courtship, you don't want to dominate the conversation but engage in the give and take. It's also important to remember the most important aspects, which is another similarity. Keep in mind; you don't need to know every single detail. You want to keep the engagement and maintain it through the entire experience.

This helps learn more about the friend you're looking to forge the friendship with and establish that bond and trust. Just like in a relationship, the higher the bond and trust, the better and more long-lasting the friendship will be. Every relationship requires trust and a strong bond to stand the test of time. Friendships are no different and hold a strong comparison to a physical relationship in that regard.

The difference between courting a friend instead of a spouse is that the chemistry over time can still build beyond just courting. With building a relationship, the chemistry needs to build rather quickly to maintain the partner's interest. Any time that it may falter, and the courtship could end right then and there.

Friend courting can be a bit more patient for a variety of reasons. Both of you could be guarded but still want to learn more about each other, a personality clash that isn't negative but slows the process, or a choice between yourself and the friend to cool things off. It's less likely that things didn't work out, but life is getting in the way of building that bond.

As an adult, it's harder to make friends because life always throws curveballs. Whether it's your job, your social engagements, or just not enough time in the day. The life of an adult makes courting friends and building bonds an obstacle. Finding ways around these issues can be overwhelming but not impossible. You could make friends at your job, where you share a common activity, use the internet to pick up platonic relationships or re-establish bonds of the past that may have fallen off because of life getting hectic. Either way, it's worth putting in the extra work to do so because being lonely is no way to live. Even if you don't have a significant other, a friend will be there to hold you steady. You can't discount the need for a true friend as their insight and knowledge could be fruitful, and their critiques will be honest and sincere.

The importance of these friends made can't be understated. These friends will be with you for the long term and will serve fruitful in times that you'll need to be uplifted. Life will give you trials and tribulations, and you'll need these friends to help get you through those trials. Losing a loved one, going through a job loss, or experiencing heartbreak, these friends will be there to help you through it all. They'll understand the plight you went through and will empathize with your situation.

It doesn't matter what you're going through; these friends will know how to handle it. You've established enough of a bond and trust with them that they know you almost as well as you know yourself. Though that seems scary to think about now, having a person that's not your spouse know you so well, the importance of that aspect can't be taken for granted.

The reason being is because, armed with the knowledge and your trust, they're going to do everything they can to keep you safe from those looking to harm you. With the bonds you formed, they understand how important you are to them and are essentially an extended family member. They'll even evaluate those you're dating and give them a once over before you start in on the situation. If they notice anything that's out of the ordinary or will harm you before the courtship starts, they'll let you know off the bat. They'll also have your back during and after the relationship should things go south.

When in a relationship, we like to view our partners through rose-colored glasses and miss out on any faults that may have been obvious. Friends that are looking out for your best interest will find these aspects and relay them to you. They'll know what you're looking for in a spouse, and if anything goes to the contrary, they'll make it known. They'll protect you from the red flags that they see and try what they can to inform you without being rude or disrespectful.

They don't want to see any ending to the relationship, but more want you to be happy. They know you'd want the same for them in return, so they work just as hard as you would to ensure that things run smoothly. They understand the importance of finding the right one and want to ensure that you realize that same goal. This is all due to the bonds you formed in the courtship stage of the friendship. They don't want to see you go through the heartbreak of rejection, so they will help you avoid it at all costs. Unfortunately, such is life, and this isn't something you can workaround. Heartbreak will happen, and it can be crushing, to say the least.

The heartbreak issue is when you'll need them the most. Going through a break-up or rejection is hard to tackle alone. The emotional aspect alone will drive you to your core. Your friends you've bonded with will be there to pick up the pieces, lift you, and offer and criticism that'll be honest and constructive. They'll also be the eyes from the outside looking in and inform you of any changes you need to make or any issues you may have missed.

A break-up can shatter you in ways that you may not understand, and your friends you've bonded with understand this tenfold. They'll be able to read your feelings and emotions of the break-up and will do what they can to help you find yourself. Whether they come to you and try to party the sadness out, share a moment of vulnerability, or try to help you determine what led to the break-up, they will be there for you and offer the support needed to help you get through your troubling time.

Their goal is to get you back to the person you were before the rejection took place because they know who you were before then. Handling this kind of emotion can make you lose yourself instantly, causing you to think negatively about yourself. Friends that have that strong bond with you will sense this and move you away from those thoughts and feelings.

They'll continue to lift you and drive you to ways of getting you out of your funk. They'll take things they learned from the courtship stage about you and use them to bring you back to life. They'll also inform you of your strong qualities and traits and make you aware of what traits may have led to the rejection or loss. They won't be rude about these critiques, but they will be firm. It's something that's needed in times like these, and your best friends can help lead you through it. Take their criticisms to heart and use them for the next time you're back on the saddle.

You don't need a large circle of friends to achieve the bonds and friendships you want. In most cases, a smaller circle will be more beneficial. A circle too large can't benefit you as they will be more like acquaintances. They may know a little about you, but not enough to know you as a true friend should.

These true friends have close bonds with you. They view you more like family and will do anything for you. Hold on to these types and hone those skills to keep you in the same grace with them as they are with you. You don't want these bonds to slip away as they are harder to come by as your get older.

To make friends like this, it will require you to court to an extent. In many ways, it will be similar to finding a partner because of the long-haul element and wanting to be compatible with that person. Not to mention the long-term bonds and trust you're looking to build. However, keep in mind that friendships can continue to grow over time and evolve, which is why they can take more time than trying to build a relationship with a spouse.

These friends will be important to you, especially if heartbreak occurs. They will be the ones to be by your side through thick and thin. They'll help enforce the fact that it's not the end of the world and that you're not alone. Having that safety net of a true bond and friendship can do wonders for your confidence and help you heal that much faster than you would've on your own. Take the time to court and build those friendships, even if it's only one or two people. Those friends alone can help save your life, and you may not even realize it at the time.

Trust the process of the friendship courtship and use it to the best of your abilities. You never know when you'll need someone like this in your corner or if you'll be that person for a friend in your life. Either way, friends will get you through anything, and their importance can't be understated. We all have them, but how many do we have that we can truly depend on? This reason is why this process is so important. Because it shows you how to make those friends and who your friends truly are.

Chapter 8:

Love Yourself

While this doesn't seem as important to many men, loving yourself may be the key to fruitful relationships and bonds. It's almost shocking hearing it out loud, but if you can't be happy with yourself, then who can you be happy with? Knowing to love yourself is knowing what you need to be happy. In most cases, it's a self-reflection that's needed to gain that introspective.

When engaging in this deep meditation, there are several aspects to think about; mainly, what is it about myself that I feel needs to change, what I need in my life to bring about my happiness, and what can I do to achieve that happiness. Only you can answer these questions, as no spouse or friend can make you love yourself.

In finding a way to love yourself, you have to determine what brings you this happiness. Finding this aspect out requires truly looking into your activities and routines. Do these things bring the happiness you're looking for, or are they coping mechanisms for something bigger? Are these healthy habits that you can keep or bad vices that need to be let go? Will this activity or habit help me progress, or is it keeping me complacent in where I currently am? These are just a small sample of what you may ask yourself during this time.

Beyond looking at activities and routines, you also need to look at what you're truly looking for. What aspects of a person would help you achieve the goals or aspirations you're looking to achieve. What is it in a mate that you want to see in yourself or help grow from you? Will having a mate at this point make you happy, or are you just going through the motions? If the latter is the case, why do you find yourself doing these things? What is it about yourself that causes you to do these things, and are there underlying unresolved issues?

You'll need to answer these questions and then some to love yourself and move forward. Finding that true happiness with yourself is important because if you can't love yourself, how can you love someone else? No one wants to be with a person who doesn't see themselves in a positive light. You have to make the necessary decisions and take the steps needed to love yourself.

As you make these decisions on what makes you happy, it's up to you to decide what to maintain. Loving yourself means growing as an individual to love others. It starts with finding things about yourself that you love and determining if those things are positive or negative traits. This point of self-reflection will be one of the hardest moments you can endure. It requires you to look deep into yourself and find your truest form of happiness.

As you examine your activities and routines, you may run into things you've done for years. They've become who you are as a person or synonymous with your personality. From here, you need to determine if it's a positive trait or a negative trait. Though it makes you happy and maybe something you're used to doing, it may not necessarily be good for you. Is it truly worth holding on to just for selfish reasons? Is this keeping you from progressing as a person?

If the answer is yes to the last question, maybe evaluate what that truly means to you and if it's only a coping mechanism. You have to know how to distinguish between harmless habits and bad vices. It's not constructive to your character; then it's time to let it go. Coping and complacency is not happiness; it's covering an underlying problem. You don't want to confuse these two aspects as it can lead to confusion. Determining the difference between them will also take some true self-reflection.

You have to determine the difference between coping and happiness. Though these aspects can seem similar, there are several differences. With happiness, it's a feeling that happens when you do something. It's not necessarily an action that can trigger it, but a memory, a person, or an action can cause the feeling. When we start attributing happiness to actions is when it starts to seep into coping.

You attach yourself to things that would make you happy and pull you from whatever funk you're in. Once you place your activities and actions into this perspective, you'll begin to see part of what's holding you back and why you are doing what you're doing.

Now, that doesn't mean giving up everything about you, just the negative connections. You don't want to be down on yourself or have things that don't help you move and grow. You also don't want to be stuck in a coping and complacency rut. Complacency doesn't allow for any growth, and you get comfortable in not progressing further. You have to find these things that give you life and not take it away from you. These changes will be necessary, but only you can determine what needs to be replaced or removed.

Keep in mind; this also isn't just reserved for your personal activities and routines. The people you have in your life can play an effect on how you view yourself. Who you associate with says a lot about your attitudes towards life and how you see your future. The people you're with have a bigger impact on decisions and lifestyles than you'd expect. However, it's up to you to determine which of these individuals are working in your best interest.

In determining what else needs to be changed, you have to look at all aspects of your courtships and friendships and look inside yourself. By this, we mean looking at the friends you're building these friendships with and the types of individuals you're courting for relationships. Who you are courting or befriending can tell you a lot about how you feel about yourself. The old saying goes, you are what you attract.

With friends, if you're adding people to your circle who aren't building you up or doing anything to gain for themselves, then they're a reflection of how you feel about yourself. You can't move forward with friends that don't have your best interests at heart. You have to look inside yourself to determine what it is that's bringing these types of friends around.

The same thing goes with finding a significant other. We all want to be with someone who will complete us and help mold us into our best selves. However, this isn't always the case, and we tend to falter in this category. Sometimes we find partners that are toxic to us and our way of life, but we can't see it at the time. By the time it's noticeable, it's too late, and we're in too deep. It's a sad state of affairs, but again, it boils down to how you view yourself.

In both of these instances, you have to take a look at yourself and see why you're attracting these types of people. Are there underlying insecurities? Maybe it's a behavioral issue that you need to address. Maybe there's something more to this story than what's known. Either way, this situation needs to be addressed. Having toxic people around you will dig at your confidence and emotions and cause more stress than necessary. Why would you want this in your life?

This is when you have to determine who is important in your life. If there are people in it that are there to keep you down, then you need to cut them out—just like in courting, ending relationships requires a process. However, if you're looking to love yourself and move forward, getting those types of people out of your life needs to happen and soon.

You'll be able to tell which of your friends are toxic, even through the rose-colored glasses. These are individuals who aren't there to help you. It may seem that way at first, but mannerisms and actions will dictate things in a different light. Be aware of these instances and use your active listening techniques and cues while you all are together.

Changes in attitude, actions, and tone all play a factor as well. If you notice the tone from these individuals is more negative than positive, then you need to remove these people. You can't have people in your life that are holding you back from your true self. You have to let them go no matter how important they were to you.

The same process has to be with significant others. Often, we choose to get into toxic relationships, even if we don't notice fully in the courtship stage. We try to minimize any cons they may have to get what we want from the person we think we need to be with. This thought process is another determination of how we view ourselves.

Some people court significant others that may have good intentions but are hiding underlying uses for you. Some of them you won't recognize, which as a human is easy to miss. However, some individuals are knowingly fraternizing with toxic personalities for a variety of reasons. These reasons are normally irrational and have to deal with fighting personal demons, or underlying issues never extinguished. It can be hard to come to this conclusion, especially with a significant other, but knowing will free you from any extra stress and heartache that comes with it.

These toxic traits are noticeable upon realization, similar to in your friend's circle. You'll notice instances of changed behavior that may not have been seen before. They're not as attentive as they once were, or the interest has wained for reasons unknown. They start taking advantage of situations and instances or playing on emotional ticks that they know you have. It's a game of emotional chicken, and they're looking to break you down to a lower version of yourself. These games can weigh heavily on your confidence and mental stability. Not to mention the added stress and anxiety that can pay a toll on a physical health capacity.

You can't allow instances like these to make you lose yourself, and allowing the games to continue will only lead to such. You'll feel like it'll hurt, and it will for a little bit, but the long run of improved mental health and self-love is much better than being tied down to a partner that isn't building you up. This is another process to being in love

with yourself. Knowing the worth that you have and not allowing partners to prey on your weaknesses.

Before you can love anyone, you have to learn to love yourself. Take the time you need to heal and become one with your feelings and emotions about who you are. After a loss, it can be hard to do so and fall into a state of depression. Rejection is hard, of course, but you can't let it become who you are. Part of that is knowing it's not the end of the world, and it's not all your fault. You're worthy of love, and you'll get it if you maintain positivity.

This includes keeping a positive circle of friends that have your best interest. Keeping people around who drag you down only serves to hurt you in the end and will affect how you view yourself. You are the company you keep, and if your company is dirty, you will be as well. Keep this in mind with your choice of partners as they can also be toxic, and you may not realize it at the time or even after the break-up. It takes knowing yourself and your worth to find these things out.

Don't allow anyone, including yourself, to doubt the worth that you have in this world. You're worthy of your happy ending, and you will find it. You have to be willing to love yourself enough to continue the fight forward and keep the friends and inner circle who won't allow you to give it up.

Chapter 9:

Know Your Feelings

Part of loving yourself is also being able to pinpoint your triggers. These traits can be for your emotions, whether happy, sad, angry, or depressed. You'll need to get in touch with your feelings and determine how to handle them in the best possible manner.

Getting a handle on your feelings will be difficult. Depending on your trait, you may rarely emote at all. Having that particular trait may come off as cold and give the wrong impression you're not trying to convey. It boils down to your personality, as if you are introverted or extroverted, that will play a factor in determining feelings.

Being introverted is keeping all of your emotions and feelings inside. You don't tend to open up to many people, and it's harder to form bonds because of it. You also may have issues in determining your true feelings because of these issues. With them being hard to express, they can be hard to diagnose. In this time, you have to look at your range of emotions and determine your feelings behind them. Once you're able to diagnose your true feelings, you'll be able to understand them better.

You have to know your breaking points and what causes you to change your moods. What is it that truly makes you tick? Determining these moments requires you to look at points in your life where you may have experienced these emotions. As an introvert, it's more or less realizing when the instance happened and how you internalized it. As an introvert, you try not to show emotion, but you do still feel it. It's looking into the moment that this happened and learning how you realized it happened.

For example, sadness is a pretty simple emotion to figure out, but it can also slip into depression. Before it gets to that point, you want to be able to pinpoint the moment you were just sad. What caused the trigger, what did you do to deal with the emotional charge, and how did you internalize it. If it evolved into depression, when did this moment happen, and how did we get to this point. You have to normalize yourself with your feelings to move forward in any instance in courtship and self-help.

Extroverts express their emotions on their sleeve, so it's easier to diagnose any emotion. The issue with extroverts is that they can sometimes give confusion with their emotions. With an extrovert's expressive nature, misunderstandings about what they're expressing can occur. What you believe may be happiness could actually be complacency or sadness.

The reason is that extroverts are just as good at hiding their emotions because they can express a variety. What they're showing isn't an emotionless void or even trying to avoid having a feeling. Instead, they're masking their true feelings by expressing a different one.

The key with extroverts is that they know their true emotions and can be in tune with them if they choose to be. It's a skill that few people have and can hone over time. Where extroverts lose sight is that, like introverts, they're guarded about their emotions which is why they choose to replace them with a different one. Unlike introverts, who thrive on not showing any emotion, extroverts have to show some form of it.

For example, an extroverted person loves to be out and about, even when they aren't feeling their best. They won't bring that emotion out with them even though that's what they feel. They'll find ways to establish showing a different emotion, use coping ways to maintain it, and continue being the life of the party. They know their true feelings, but they aren't dealing with them, only solving half the problem. It's willfully naivety to the situation at hand to maintain a certain look.

In both traits, you see the issues where knowing your feelings brings about an issue, an absence of showing your true feelings. Doing this can hurt you in various ways, and not being in tune with your true feelings leads to many unwanted scenarios and possible misunderstandings. You have to know and understand your true feelings and handle them in a mentally healthy way. Not doing so will affect you in the long term and could factor in other aspects of your social life.

Not knowing and trusting your instincts and feelings will leave you with poor confidence and a circle of people in your life that may not work in your best interest. You're willing to accept more than you normally would to avoid having to deal with the fallout of your emotions. You'll accept people who take advantage and tear you down instead of building you up. Your choice of partners will also be affected as you may not choose those who serve your best interests. You have to know and be in tune with your feelings in all aspects to avoid these pitfalls.

Beyond courtships and relationships, setting up friendships and acquaintances requires knowing your feelings. How you feel around a person, and your true emotional reactions will determine if they will be a close friend, an acquaintance, or a one-time meeting. It'll be vibes, attitudes, and cues that you'll look for, plus one other very important aspect.

You'll know the difference just based on your vibes felt and gut instinct. Knowing your feelings is a huge contributor to that. If the vibe feels right, you're more likely to continue the friendship and reveal more about yourself. The trust factor is heightened, and the bond continues to form. This is all based on an initial instinct. You trusted your feelings and led you in the right direction in making a lasting bond.

In the same vein, you'll have the same vibes when it comes to acquaintances and one-time meeting individuals. You'll feel the vibes of uneasiness or allow only a little of yourself to be involved in the social engagement. You'll feel guarded about your most personal aspects but may give enough to suffice for the moment or keep them at arm's length. Your gut instinct is telling you do not fully trust the situation and maybe re-evaluate pursuing this friendship.

Gut instinct can serve you very in the friendship aspect, and it's something that we all have. Where it lacks is honing this skill to match knowing our feelings or listening to those instincts. It's imperative to keep these skills as sharp as possible. Beyond finding friends and knowing your limitations and trigger points, you can use this skill to determine if a partner is worth pursuing or handling a break-up should things go south.

In terms of the courtship, gut instinct and feelings will help determine if the pursuit is truly worth it. While there may be aspects that you like about this person, your instincts may say otherwise. They may not work in your best interest for a multitude of reasons.

Many times in the courtship stage, we tend to allow aspects and red flags to slip by. We may also allow ourselves to continue to fall for a certain type of individual that isn't healthy. This reason could be an absence of knowing what feeling you're missing or knowing this is happening to achieve that feeling negatively. Either way, it does nothing to help the situation and causes effects on your confidence.

You have to know your feelings in this situation and speak up when things aren't going the way you feel they should be. Not doing so will open you to either being walked all over or accepting situations you normally wouldn't. Be in tune with your feelings and make sure your partner knows them as well, so you're not wasting each other's time. It'll save both of you a lot of trouble and you a lot of stress.

Concerning a break-up, knowing your feelings is just as crucial. It's an important aspect because it lets you know how you deal with the initial rejection and deal with things from here. As we've stated previously, there are positives and negatives to what happens from here. How well you know your feelings and how to maintain them will be the catalyst of the outcomes.

You can take rejection in a variety of ways. How well you choose to handle it takes knowing exactly how you feel after the rejection or break-up. Most men try to act like they aren't hurt after rejection and attempt to do anything to avoid the defeated feeling. They ignore the initial feeling and try to replace it.

Though this acknowledges your feelings, it's not a healthy way to deal with the situation. You're not allowing yourself to heal from the situation and, in turn, open yourself up to more hurt and heartache. So you may know what your feelings are, but you don't know how to deal with them.

It takes time to heal and deal with the emotions that will come in waves. Knowing your feelings, and owning them from the start, will make getting through the rough period easier. It'll also help build your confidence when getting back into the dating world and knowing your worth so you don't fall into the same habits.

You can also choose to stay in the funk and not get a handle on the down feeling. You stay forever bitter after the break-up or rejection and come up with irrational generalizations based on the experience. It doesn't acknowledge your feelings, but places blame on an outside source to justify your feelings. Not just for the situation at hand but future situations.

Instead of dealing with and knowing how you feel, you go with the avoidance approach. This unhealthy choice allows you to continue to be vague with your feelings and find other ways to excuse where you are. You don't want to heal, which stunts where you are as a person and leads to the generalizations that you use to rationalize your thought process.

This is a slippery slope to place yourself on as it could hinder all other aspects of your life. You'll refuse to take responsibility for even the simplest of things because you don't want to own up to your feelings on the matter. It's a willful naivety that's self-imposed but only does harm to your psyche.

Meanwhile, the positive way of handling your rejection is to take your feelings to

account and know how you truly feel. Is there a feeling of regret and anger, or did you understand why the break-up happened? Did this break-up cause a rift anywhere else within you? Do you think you can handle getting through this on your own, or will you need help doing so?

You'll do your best to answer these questions, as well as others that may roam through your mind. It would be best if you had this time to answer, find that closure and heal. Knowing your feelings and using that to help ease the pain will make the healing process that much better. It'll help you diagnose what you need to do, how you need to handle the situation, and how to move forward, so you don't have this situation again.

Now, just like in other aspects of rebuilding and self-reflection, professional help may also need to be an option. Relationship counselors or mental health experts can help you get in touch with your feelings. Please don't view this as a weakness by any means because everyone has different ways of fixing their problem. Reaching out and knowing what you need is part of acknowledging your feelings. You're aware that it's hard for you to emote and find the right feeling to express. You're taking those steps to better yourself and get more in tune with yourself on an emotional level.

Knowing your feelings and being in tune with yourself emotionally is extremely important in growing as a person and forming relationships and courtships. Though it is important to consider the other party's feelings in the courting phase, you have to take yourself into account as well.

If you have your feelings intact, you're less willing to allow certain things around you. You don't want the stress of the anxiety of unwanted instances, and you're aware of where they come from. You'll also pinpoint when certain individuals aren't in your best interest and only want you for certain aspects.

Not having this trait in tune can and will harm you in the worst of ways. It came to permeate through your social settings and life choices. You have to know your feelings and own up to them. Trying to hide, avoid, or circumvent is just putting a bandaid on the issue. You have to take the initiative and do what you need to to have a handle on yourself.

No one will do this for you. You can only handle this yourself. It's going to require you to look into yourself and reflect. Not just on your personality or mannerisms, but also on your habits and individuals you allow around you. You'll have to ask why you do these things and if it's an act of being complacent. Are you truly in tune with yourself and your instincts, and do you trust them? Answering these questions won't be easy, and it may even get uncomfortable, but in the end, it's necessary to know more about yourself and to progress forward.

Chapter 10:

Take Things Seriously

This bit of wisdom may come across as self-explanatory, but it's highly important to take things seriously regarding finding your perfect match.

Friendships and bonds are important, but there's no better feeling than finding your better half. Knowing that you've made the deep connection with the one you're looking for can change your whole outlook on life. However, one must remember that you can't take this moment for granted, and you'll need to work just as hard to maintain what you've made.

If you've found the one that you're looking for and the feeling is mutual, now is not the time to sit back and rest on the foundation you've built. It's great to have gotten to this point, as this is what you're looking to achieve, but that doesn't mean that the journey is over. You've made it past the courtship stage and into the relationship stage. At this point, you have to work twice as hard to maintain what you have and build what you need to build.

In the courtship stage, many instances were overlooked or seen as a cute quirk, but over time these small things will build up and begin to lose their luster. You'll have to find ways to keep things fresh and exciting as well as, by this point, your partner may feel they know enough about you or know your routines. You'll have to also be in tune with how they feel in the relationship and do your best to keep that going.

We mentioned strong traits and weaknesses earlier in this text. During this phase, your weaknesses may shine through more so than your strengths. The reason being is because the time has been put in to know more about each other. At this point, there are no real surprises, or there shouldn't be. This aspect means there may be certain things about you that may rear their ugly head. Now, it doesn't necessarily mean you need to change, but it may be a good idea to minimize these as much as possible.

Your spouse will never ask you to change who you are because that's what attracted them to you. However, there may be things they'll ask you to compromise on. If you have minimized any habits or vices in courtship, they'll come to light in the "honeymoon" stage. If your partner is not keen on them, then these sacrifices will happen.

It's up to you to understand that if you want this relationship to foster, you may need to make some changes to your lifestyle. Take these moments very seriously, as if you choose not to make these changes or at least make an effort, you run the risk of losing the mate you worked so hard for. Take your vices and habits into perspective and ensure you're both on the same page regarding them. You have to show that maturity of wanting to share all of yourself will go a long way to build that long-term relationship.

Keep in mind that you'll have to have these same thoughts regarding your spouse. You want to do this for the long haul, which means being cool with their habits and vices. If there's something they're doing that you're not cool with, you have to let them know and see how they react. They'll be willing to make those strides to change, or they'll remain the same. You do have the right to voice your opinion, and you're encouraged to speak up when something bothers you.

Just keep in mind the risk you run with this aspect. If they aren't willing to change for you, you may have to deal with the vice or lose the relationship. The changes they make may not also go as quickly as you'd like or how you'd want. These aspects must be taken into account if you want things to continue to run smoothly. This give and take will be important to the relationship's long-term success and are important to keep things exciting within the relationship.

During this time of taking things seriously, you have to stay in tune with your partner's emotions. The honeymoon stage of the courtship will be happy for the most part, but again, the newness of the relationship will start to run thin. You'll have to continue to engage your partner and keep them interested. You won't be able to use the same stories, and you'll need to create new memories and moments to maintain the freshness of the relationship.

To do this, speak with your partner and engage in ways to continue to make those moments. Their input is highly important as it requires effort from both of you to make this last. However, you're showing that you're taking this seriously because you want them actively involved. Your goal is to include them in your life in every facet, so engaging their likes and wants is just as important.

Now, don't lose yourself in doing this, as you'll still need to stand your ground on things you would like, but sharing your likes and wanting to mesh them with your partner's vision is a huge step in the right direction. It shows you're willing to merge your worlds and think about the future you guys will have. Your partner will be more willing to continue that engagement and further work to make shared goals a reality.

In keeping them involved with your goals, it's important to set posts for goals. You don't want to remain stagnant, and spontaneity is what will also help keep things fresh. Though having a routine is nice and shows some maturity, you don't want to fall into the same things all the time. You'll have to mix it up ever so often and throw in something new to keep the freshness alive. Sometimes a surprise dinner or vacation, maybe a special gift just because, or even something as small as an intimate massage done yourself, are all things that show that you're bringing something different.

Now again, this doesn't mean to change everything about you. It's adding to the toolbox that you've already made. Your spouse loves who you are and doesn't want to change you, but showing that you're willing to add new things and not rest on what you already have is a sign that you're willing to make this work for more than just the moment. You want this moment to last for a lifetime and growing yourself to do so.

Anyone can stop growing as a spouse and use what they already have, but you're showing your spouse that you're willing to go the extra mile. You want her to know that you want them and will do what's needed to maintain that interest. Your spouse will not only love but cherish and respect this action and will reciprocate the action. They'll be willing to try new things and even add to their toolbox to keep you with them. It's another addition to the give-and-take element of taking the relationship seriously.

When you find the one that you truly want, and the courtship stage goes according to how you want, know that this isn't the end of the journey. There's going to be more that you'll need to do to maintain the longevity of your new relationship. You won't be able to rest on the things that brought you to the dance but maintain and overstep them. You have to go beyond what you did during the courtship stage.

You have to stay in tune with your partner's emotions and respect their opinions on and about the relationship. Knowing what they're looking for and staying in that lane as far the relationship is concerned will work wonders in the longevity. You don't want to lose yourself in this aspect and become a doormat, but you have to understand that this has become a partnership. This is a give-and-take situation now, and you'll need to listen and empathize as well as understand and mend.

You also have to continue to be the person you were when the relationship started. This issue means keeping your strengths intact and making your partner aware of and cool with your vices and habits. If there are any habits that they're not keen on at this point, you have to consider sacrificing them completely or making ways to amend them. You'll also have to consider this with your partner and determine if you're ok with them and their faults. You both may have to make sacrifices to make this work, but if it's worth the long-term investment, you'll do so.

You'll also have to have some form of spontaneity. Though your partner will never ask you to change yourself for them, it doesn't hurt to add new things to the playbook. This aspect goes hand in hand with being in tune with emotions. If you notice boredom or their interest starting to wain, do something different. Add something new and see if the spark returns even for a moment.

You have to do these things to take your relationship seriously. You've worked this hard to get to this point, and you're at the light at the end of the courtship tunnel. You'll have to do just a little more work to stay in that light for a while longer.

Conclusion

Thank you for choosing to read *Look At Her Shoes: Even In Loss, A Love Story Is Worth Living*. Let's hope it was informative and able to provide you with all of the tools you need to achieve your goals, whatever they may be.

The next step is to use the skills and ideas learned in this book to the best of your abilities. With the knowledge you've gained, here's to progress in your journey of courtships, relationships, friendships, and forming personal bonds. Be attentive to your relatability, confidence, chemistry, time, self-love, feelings, and seriousness to the tasks.

Confidence itself will be a huge factor, so it's imperative to develop this trait. You'll need this to either make the moves needed to begin courtship or move on from the failed attempt. Confidence can make or break your abilities in both aspects. Be sure to find ways to keep it as high as possible and surround yourself with those who can help with that boost.

Remember, even if things don't go according to plan, there's nothing in the path of finding your true love. It's a minor obstacle on a longer path that'll be worth the experiences in the long run. Don't allow those obstacles to deter you and learn from the inconvenience at hand. Being armed with this knowledge will make things more fruitful and perhaps lead to a better thought process for yourself and those around you.

Finally, if you found this book useful in any way, a review on Amazon is always appreciated!